TOM HANKS

A CAREER IN ORBIT

TOM HANKS

A CAREER IN ORBIT

DAVID QUINLAN

B.T. BATSFORD LTD LONDON

Printed in Singapore
for the Publishers B.T. Batsford
583 Fulham Road
London SW6 5BY

ISBN 0 7134 8073 4

Acknowledgments

The author and publisher would like to thank the
Kobal Collection for provision of the illustrations
used on the cover and on pages 2, 7, 16-17, 19, 23,
33, 34, 39, 42, 43, 44, 55, 56, 58, 59, 63, 68, 70, 71,
73, 81, 83, 88.
Thanks also to Ted Heslin for helpful editorial advice.

CONTENTS

It was a typical long, hot, dry California summer. But Amos Hanks was irritable and discontented. He was a good chef, but he just couldn't seem to make a go of running his own place. A talent for cookery and a head for business didn't seem to run together in the Hanks family.

And now Janet was pregnant again. Two hungry mouths already to feed and another on the way. His failure to settle down was putting a strain on the marriage. He didn't look forward to going home to a household where a fight was more likely than not. And his back hurt. Amos put that down to long hours of working on his feet.

10 9 8 7 6 5 4 3 2 1

THE 'BURBS

They had had a boy and a girl already and Amos fancied the new arrival would be another boy. They'd give it another good solid name to follow Lawrence and Sandra. Amos favoured Thomas or James...

July 1956. In not-too-distant Hollywood, a teen idol called Elvis Presley was making his first movie, *Love Me Tender*. But, although a giant of the music industry, he would never quite reach the same status at the box-office as the dark-haired boy born to Amos and Janet Hanks on 9 July.

At the Venice Film Festival, 1995

For the new arrival, early homes in Concord and Oakland proved to be the first of many, as Amos Hanks trudged from town to town in search of culinary success. Most of their stopping places were, like Concord and Oakland, satellite suburbs of San Francisco: in the next few years, Fremont, San Mateo, Pleasanton, Alameda and San Leandro all provided temporary homes for the itinerant Hankses.

In time, Amos also ventured northwards, to Redding and Sacramento. But nothing lasted long. Sometimes Amos ran a small coffee shop, sometimes dinner houses, sometimes restaurants inside hotels. But whenever he tired of combining chef's and manager's jobs or his back protested at the long hours that left his wife and children on their own until late at night, Amos would pack home and family into a U-haul trailer and move on.

His three children were excited by his next job, as the family crossed the state line, and Amos landed a position as chef to a casino in the Nevada city of Reno, haven of gambling and divorce. The new apartment was a step up in class from what the family had been used to. But they weren't there long.

Like his career and his health, Amos's marriage was rocky. Shortly after the birth of their fourth child, James (Jim), Amos and Janet decided to split up. Amos kept the three older children and continued drifting around the Los Angeles area, his latest stamping ground. Taking baby Jim with her, Janet moved nearly 400 miles to the north to a modest wooden bungalow in Red Bluff, not far from one of their former homes in Redding.

Sandra, the eldest Hanks child, found herself at ten pretty much the mother of the family. 'Dad', she remembers, 'was still working long hours and nights in the restaurant business. So we took care of the place, fed ourselves, did our own laundry and pretty much learned self-sufficiency.

'On the odd summer night when Dad had time off, he'd

throw a mattress in the back of the pick-up. Tom, Larry and I would sit in the back and we'd go to a drive-in movie. Dad never bothered to check what films were on – we'd just go.'

Amos and Janet Hanks had raised their children in the Catholic faith. All that changed when Amos married his second wife, a Mormon woman with five children of her own. Said Tom, then six; 'we soon found things were different.

'My first stepmother was somewhat flaky. Her love of the Mormon Church was just one of the reasons I think Dad left her. Dad did kind of rebel against it though. She's not a Mormon now. She's probably into astrology or something.

'Drawing a picture of our house and family at school in those days', remembers Tom, 'was tricky. I ran out of places to put people and eventually stuck them on the roof. But when that marriage broke up, I never saw those people again.'

When Amos found himself out of work once more, the kids were farmed out to an aunt. Sandra, Larry and Tom lived in the house with her while their father slept in the back yard in his battered old trailer.

Amos got work in a local restaurant, but happiness wasn't on the menu for the children. The aunt who had taken them in proved to be a fanatical follower of the fundamentalist Church of the Nazarenes.

Recalls Tom: 'We weren't allowed to watch TV. There were long lists of rules and awfully long prayers. I sure had exposure to a lot of ways of worshipping God.'

In the privacy of his bedroom, Tom became fascinated with the progress of the US space programme. His favourite toy was a bendable, posable astronaut called Major Matt Mason. 'He was made of rubber like Gumby and he had a space helmet', recalls Hanks. 'If you played with him too

"We weren't allowed to watch TV. There were long lists of rules and awfully long prayers."

Toy Story: Woody, Buzz Lightyear, Mr Potatohead and some bucket soldiers. That's Tom on the left

much, the wire inside his arm would break and he could no longer pose that part. It was kind of frustrating.'

And there was occasional relief from the tyranny of his aunt. 'Although my parents no longer talked to one another', says Tom, 'I went up to my mother's house every holiday –Thanksgiving, Christmas, Easter.

'I consider Red Bluff my home in a lot of ways. You could hop on a bike and go down to the river and stop at the store for ice cream on the way back.' Janet, on the second of her four marriages, and working for a property management company, did what she could to make up for his lost childhood.

'At Easter we'd paint Easter eggs together', she recalls. 'Then I'd hide the eggs around the house and in the garden. The reward for finding one was 50 cents.

'At Christmas we tried to make it as traditional as possible with turkey and the trimmings. Tom had a Christmas stocking with his name on it hung over the fireplace.

'He was always entertaining. During his visits he'd turn a sock into a puppet and put on a little show. When he said something cute and adults reacted to it with amusement, he'd repeat it endlessly, milking the line for all it was worth. Tom had a natural love of the limelight.'

For Jim Hanks, his brother's visits were less of a pleasure. 'It may seem unlikely now,' he says, 'but Tom was a bit of a bruiser in those days, always beating me up. His favourite trick was to lock me in my wardrobe.

'I'd scream but, to be honest, it was a relief when he locked me up. It meant he wasn't beating me.' The two brothers would remain distant until the late 1980s.

Soon, Amos Hanks took his children away from the aunt they hated and hit the road again. With Amos working until 10 pm, the kids were left to fend for themselves once more. Dinner on a good night might be burned steak and instant mash.

Allowed to settle at school, Tom rapidly became the class clown. 'I was in second grade,' he says, 'when I found I could make people laugh by acting the fool. The night before, my older brother, Larry, had done something funny at dinner. I repeated it at school. I don't even remember now what I did. You know how, when kids are a year older than you, they seem like giants? Well, I made the giants laugh.'

Back home, life was less fun. Amos's back pains – in reality a kidney problem –3 had grown more frequent and were serious enough to force him to take time off work. 'Sometimes,' says Tom, 'Dad was really sick. He'd be lying there unconscious, semi-comatose, you know, hardly there. All that you could do for him was to mop up his face with a wash rag. That does something to you that you don't forget.'

Wifely care for Amos, however, was again at hand. He met and married a Chinese woman, Frances, who added her own three children to the Hanks household.

The Hanks children didn't like it. Not one little bit. Says Tom: 'We'd lived like little savages for two-and-a-half years. Called our own shots. Suddenly this woman was telling us what to do. I mean, we weren't about to start washing our hair and making our beds: we'd been raised like lion cubs. This person was trying to make us into a suburban-type family, which wasn't what we wanted.'

Adds Sandra: 'After spending so much time on our own, looking after each other, it came as a shock to us, suddenly living with these Chinese stepsisters.

'On top of that, Dad's Chinese wife was really very traditional. We went from a steady diet of pizza to being served Chinese dishes at every meal.' It was more than 13-year-old Sandra could stand. She ran away to live with her mother and Jim in Red Bluff.

Larry and Tom found themselves little more than lodgers in their own father's house. Says Tom: 'We just kind of

Making the giants laugh – **Big**

exorcised ourselves from the regular routine of living in the house, and we became two households in one.

'It was upstairs and downstairs, because our house was built on the side of a hill. So the top floor was the main living area, and the bottom floor was where Larry and I lived.'

Still, there was now television and the NASA space programme, both of which fuelled Tom's fascination with space travel. In 1966, the pioneering TV series *Star Trek* started, and Tom was soon hooked. He became a lifetime fan.

Back in the twentieth century, Tom followed just as avidly the exploits of NASA astronauts. Pretty soon his bedroom was looking like a miniature version of Mission Control. He built models of the spacecraft and filled scrapbooks full of information.

'I was intensely aware of the space programme from Apollo 7 onwards', says the man who 30 years later would himself play one of America's most famous astronauts. 'I knew what all the flights were doing. I knew where they were going. I knew the crews. I would read about it in the *San Francisco Chronicle*. I would run home from school to see what was happening whenever a moonshot was scheduled.'

"I was intensely aware of the space programme from Apollo 7 onwards."

In the upstairs household, his father's condition was deteriorating. With no health insurance and the fear that his children would be taken from him if he had to spend a period in hospital, Amos Hanks had worked on through the pain. None too soon he checked into a charity hospital. Almost the first thing he did was lapse into unconsciousness.

Amos's kidney problem was at last diagnosed and treated. But it seemed too late for any permanent cure. Says Tom: 'Dad almost died that first time in hospital. Over the next seven or eight years, I can remember Larry and I going to see him four or five more times in hospital, each time thinking this was finally it.' Amos became an expert at cheating death, but the battle was ongoing, and the Hanks children's youth was marred by the strain of constantly being on the verge of losing their father.

Hanks' wife Rita Wilson

Next page: Bill Paxton, Kevin Bacon and Hanks aboard *Apollo 13*

10 9 8 7 6 5 4 3 2 1

MISCHIEF

'No', says Tom, 'I have no affection at all for the late sixties. The sky was full of helicopters dropping gas on people at Berkeley. Kennedy was dead, Nixon was corrupt. The US was fighting in Vietnam. A guy called Huey Newton was in jail for a couple of murders. Nobody seemed to care that we'd just landed on the moon. I just figured the world was going to hell in a handbag.

'What I remember most about those years', he says, 'is how confused I felt. I couldn't figure out how anything worked... my house, my parents, my school and especially girls.

'In many ways, I was younger than my years. I still liked playing with soldiers and toy planes, inventing incredible adventures. I was right in the middle of the sexual revolution – but I didn't know it yet.' He would remain a virgin until he went to university, where a sexual relationship would prove his undoing.

For the moment, though, at Skyline High School in Oakland, Tom found religion coming back into his life. He admits that, at this stage of his development, he 'conducted my own theological search for a while. Very conservative, very Bible-oriented. Two services – Sunday morning and Sunday evening. It beat smoking pot.'

Vietnam sequence from **Forrest Gump**

Says Sandra Hanks: 'He had a semi-righteousness that went along with being 15, as if he had seen the light and the rest of us were in the dark. I think he got heavily involved with the church not so much for religion as the activities. It was a non-threatening environment with lots to do.'

It was through a Christian Fellowship group at Skyline that Tom became involved with his first serious girlfriend, Carol Wiele. 'Until then', he admits, 'I was death with women – absolutely the strike-out king. I was totally crippled when it came to confidence with the opposite sex.'

'He was goofy,' remembers Carol, 'but he really cared about people. We went on a double date to the senior prom. Tom looked great in his tuxedo and tried hard to be romantic. He bought me a lovely corsage and we had a candlelit dinner. Soon after, though, we stopped dating and became just friends. I don't know why, but dating Tom just didn't work out.'

Tom, though, had discovered another kind of passion. 'I took a drama class that determined the rest of my life. In this one course of ten weeks, we saw five completely different sorts of theatre. I fell in love, not just with acting but with the theatre. The whole experience.'

His subsequent college dramatics were highlighted not so much by interpretations of Shakespeare as by an exuberant, scene-stealing performance in a production of *South Pacific*, complete with grass skirt and coconut bra. Onlookers claimed that the tattoo of a ship on his stomach looked as though it were really sailing.

Holidays were often spent touring round church groups with the Christian Fellowship drama section, putting on plays. On one such trip, Tom stayed with Bertie McColloch, a single mother with three children, one of whom, Spike, suffered from Bell's Palsy.

'He would talk to the kids for hours', she recalls, 'and gently tease Spike, and make him laugh at himself. Spike was so self-conscious, he didn't even want to go to school or out to play. But Tom convinced him through his sense of humour that there was nothing to be ashamed of. He changed my boy's life forever.'

Graduating from Skyline in 1974, Hanks went on to Sacramento State University. Called back home, he found his father in the midst of another crisis. A donor kidney was found to replace the one that had failed.

Amos was hurried to a San Francisco hospital for the transplant that seemed to be his last hope. But his body rejected the new kidney. The Hanks family faced a tense wait while the hospital hunted for another.

"I only had a couple of years to sow my wild oats."

The second operation was a success and somehow Amos pulled through. Tom was by his side, finding it difficult to forge a common bond. Years later he tried to explain. 'It's a curious thing. I lived with my Dad the longest out of all of us, but I'm probably the most opposite to him in terms of personality. He was a good guy, but he was no good at communicating. He wasn't able to put things into perspective for me or for any of his other three kids.'

While Tom returned to university, his older brother and sister had begun to build their own careers, Larry as an entomologist and Sandra on the way to a successful business supplying newsreel clips to TV stations.

Meantime, Tom was into less worthy activities at Sacramento. He was smoking marijuana and dabbling in cocaine, while continuing his drama studies. He had also discovered girls and how to get them into bed. 'But I only had a couple of years to sow all my wild oats. At 21 I'd be married.'

The wife-to-be was Susan Dillingham, a pretty university student who had already done some acting under the name

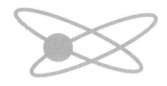

Samantha Lewes. 'It was a college relationship', says Tom, 'with the two of us going off to work in the theatre, discovering Samantha was pregnant and marrying after our son Colin was born.

'A child was the last thing we needed at that time, but there we were, our version of what my own parents had been through.'

'Tom had gained experience behind the scenes as a carpenter, stage manager, scenic artist and lighting technician.'

Bachelor Party: the bachelors

Before he dropped out ('I actually sort of dribbled out') of university, Tom had gained experience behind the scenes as a carpenter, stage manager, scenic artist and lighting technician. 'But,' he says, 'I soon discovered the most magical place to be was on the stage.'

So it was as an actor that he auditioned for director Vincent Dowling in 1977. 'He just turned up with several others', Dowling recalls. 'When I got home that afternoon, I told my wife there was one kid there who had star quality: Tom.' The consequence was that Tom got a role in Dowling's production of *The Cherry Orchard*, as well as an introduction to the Shakespeare Festival near Cleveland, Ohio.

Tom stayed with the Shakespeare company for two years, working both behind the scenes as stage manager, and acting 18 different roles. None of them, however, were as leading characters. It was great experience, but journeyman work and, by the end of 1978, Tom had resolved to try his luck in New York.

'When you've played Montano in *Othello* a couple of times,' he comments, 'let me tell you, you never want to do it again. I mean, five months being the guy who runs out at the start of the second act and asks "What from the cape can you discern at sea?" It begins to wear thin.'

'Fatherhood passed me by in a blur,' Tom has said. It was 1979 and the only money coming into the Hanks household was from unemployment benefit. Pot and cocaine had been left behind. 'It put not just me, but the people I loved in a degree of danger,' says Tom. 'So it became pretty easy to say "No more".

'I thought: "I can't be a responsible parent and do this".' Doubtless money was also a consideration.

'It was a time fraught with unhappiness,' Tom remembers. 'I was on unemployment and trying to act. Samantha was pursuing her career the best she could and take care of the baby.

'Sometimes I'd take a hundred dollars and drive from city to city looking for work. I went for the jobs that nobody else wanted.

Sometimes I'd wake up at night, go into the bathroom, look at myself in the mirror and think: "What's happened to me? My career's over before it's begun." I had periods when the black dog followed me around and I just couldn't shake him off.' There was precious little time to dote on his baby.

10 9 8 7 6 5 4 3 2 1

THE MONEY PIT

A shouting match with Shelley Long in
The Money Pit

At last, though, there was a little more work to help pay the rent and keep the landlord at bay. Tom was hired by the Riverside Shakespeare Company. And there was a (dreadful) low-budget horror film, *He Knows You're Alone*. Tom was eighth-billed as Elliot. 'It may have been bad,' he says, 'but it was the first job I had wearing regular pants, you know, as opposed to sword belts, leather jerkins and sandals.'

Tom also attempted to break into television. He auditioned several times for ABC. 'Finally I got a development deal with the company and we moved back to California.' Almost straight away, the company gave Tom his first lead. The show was called *Bosom Buddies*. Tom and Peter Scolari ventured into *Some Like It Hot* territory as two frazzled ad men who find the only place they can afford to live is a ladies' hostel. So they dress up in drag and pitch in with the girls.

The series ran for two seasons and would be Tom's first and last. 'It was like going to an aeroplane factory every day,' he says. 'You go into a big hangar and build a plane and every Friday it has to fly. Unfortunately, sometimes the wings fell off.'

Bosom Buddies, whatever its faults, did lead to other television work, including a guest spot on the popular *Happy Days*, where one of the stars was Ron Howard, who was impressed with Tom's clowning abilities. 'Tom,' he remembers, 'played a guy whom Fonzie had pushed out of a swing during childhood but who returns as a judo black belt to claim revenge. It made a lasting impression on me, he was so funny.'

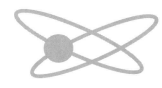

"It was the first job I had wearing regular pants."

During the run of *Bosom Buddies*, Samantha had a second child, Elizabeth, in 1981. Tom's income had picked up, and he starred in a TV movie, *Mazes and Monsters*, the following year.

'Keaton had turned down the leading role in Howard's new project, a comedy about a mermaid.'

Tom played Robbie, a university student whose fixation with a Dungeons and Dragons-type game leads him and three fellow students into real-life dangers. Canadian-made, the telefilm became a popular repeat a few years later after Tom's big-screen success.

By the end of 1982, though, that success must have seemed far away. Both Tom and Samantha were beginning to realise that they had been too young to marry. Their rows grew more frequent, especially when money was tight which, throughout 1983, it was.

Late in the year, there was the chance to audition for another film. Tom's old *Happy Days* colleague, Ron Howard, had turned director with some success. One of his early films, *Night Shift*, had made a star out of Michael Keaton. Keaton had turned down the leading role in Howard's new project, a comedy about a mermaid, which had finally landed at Disney after being rejected by other studios.

Auditioning for a supporting part, Tom impressed Howard so much that he was asked to play the starring role. The mermaid was to be played by leggy blonde Daryl Hannah and the coverage the film received ensured that life for Tom Hanks would never be the same again.

10 9 8 7 6 5 4 3 2 1

MAKING A SPLASH

A youthful-looking Hanks stars with
Daryl Hannah in **Splash**

The Disney Studio had been floundering with its live-action pictures for some time, and seemed to have lost sight of its audience. *Splash* was the first of what would be increasingly successful movies intended to capture the adult market and bring that half of the company's business into line with its cartoon successes.

Not that there isn't much that's cartoon-like about *Splash*'s storyline. Tom plays Allen Bauer who, as a boy, had fallen overboard from a ferry boat and been rescued by a young mermaid in whose presence he discovers an ability to breathe underwater.

Twenty years later, Allen returns to Cape Cod and is again rescued from drowning by the same mermaid – whom he fails to recognize. She follows him to New York, where he runs a vegetable business with his brother (John Candy). After various saucy misadventures, they fall in love (the mermaid's tail metamorphoses into legs on dry land) but the mermaid, Madison, is captured and clapped into a giant fish tank. Naturally, there's a happy ending, with Allen and his brother rescuing Madison and our happy couple swimming off together into the depths.

Tom's wage packet for the starring part in *Splash* was $70,000 – his biggest ever for a single role. The film itself took more than 500 times that figure. It was Disney's most successful live-action film for 15 years and ushered in a new era for the studio. Although Daryl Hannah as Madison the amorous mermaid was the image splashed across a thousand newspapers and magazines, she and Tom both wore out many pairs of shoes promoting the film around the world – to great success.

Tom's personal reviews couldn't have been better. *Variety* said that 'Hanks, as a bachelor in search of love, makes a fine leap from sitcom land.' Full of amusing incidentals, the film and its stars delighted the public.

Some of its scenes were shot on location in the Bahamas, where Tom developed a lifetime interest in scuba diving. 'There's a whole undiscovered world down there,' he said. 'My look of amazement in the underwater scenes was genuine.'

Suddenly studios were pursuing Tom rather than the other way round. To mark his new celebrity, he bought himself a reflector telescope to further his interest in space and astronomy.

None of these interests unfortunately were shared by Samantha. Tom found himself enjoying life away from home more than spending time with his wife. There were plenty of film offers and he accepted more of them than perhaps he should.

With Meg Ryan in **Joe versus the Volcano**

Strangely, none of the mediocrities he made over the next four years seemed to mar audiences' liking for his work or his standing in the industry.

Word of mouth about his showing in *Splash* got Tom the lead in another comedy even before the Disney film was released. *Bachelor Party*, though, was a different kettle of fish. A juvenile sex romp appealing to the lowest common denominator, it cast Tom as Rick, a happy-go-lucky bus driver whose impending wedding is imperilled both by the opposition of the girl's parents and by the sex-strewn stag spree arranged by his own friends.

Partly thanks to the public's liking for low comedy, still prevalent today, the film showed a handsome profit. Tom's personality also helped. Said *Variety*: 'Main reason to see the pic is for Hanks's performance... he's all over the place, practically spilling off the screen with an over-abundance of energy.'

Tom now enjoyed a reputation as a bright young comedy star. But the loyalty of his fans was to be severely tested by the clutch of films he now took on.

The Man With One Red Shoe (also known as *Mischief*) was a remake of a French comedy film that wasn't all that funny to begin with. Despite a great supporting cast that included Carrie Fisher and Jim Belushi, the American version has almost no laughs at all.

Tom, who rates it as his worst film, plays a violinist caught up in CIA activities. The film couldn't even get a release outside the United States, a record bettered (though not by much) by Tom's next, *Volunteers*. This was a messy-looking comedy which cast him as a spoiled playboy who joins the Peace Corps to avoid bookmaker's heavies and tries to run (or rather ruin) PC activities in the Thai jungle.

John Candy was again Tom's co-star, but the film's probably had more plays on television than it did in the cinema.

Much funnier, though disliked by the critics in

Hanks stars in
The Man With One Red Shoe

32

Volunteers:
Tom Hanks, Rita Wilson and John Candy

America, was *The Money Pit* , an updating of the classic Cary Grant comedy *Mr Blandings Builds His Dream House*. Tom and his talented co-star Shelley Long work hard to keep the comedy bubbling in this tall tale of a yuppie couple who somehow afford a country mansion almost the size of an English stately home.

It is, however, falling apart – 'We're living in a Swiss cheese with a door' they howl. The resulting antics went down better in Britain, where *Film Review* described the film as a 'full-tilt laughterhouse of domestic chaos that combines a verbally dextrous script with slapstick stunts'.

Seeking a change of pace, Tom flew to Israel to make *Every Time We Say Goodbye*, a wartime romance about an American soldier who falls in love with the daughter of a strict Sephardic Jewish family. Despite a few amusing moments early

With Cristina Marsillach in
Every Time We Say Goodbye

A confrontation with Alexander Godunov in
The Money Pit

in the film, director Moshe Mizrahi's script gave Tom and his Israeli supporting cast very little chance to engender any real feeling.

Tom flew back with a sense of foreboding and he was right: the film quickly dropped from sight everywhere it was shown. Tom would later say, only half-jokingly, that he had made this string of flops 'to get out of the house'.

It was true, though, that things were no less gloomy on the home front. Thanks to his increased earnings, Tom and Samantha had moved to a much larger property in North Hollywood's fashionable Addison Street. Its walk soon reverberated with the sounds of angry voices, as the couple's marriage deteriorated to the point where it seemed they could only communicate on shouting terms.

To their friends, divorce seemed inevitable.

10 9 8 7 6 5 4 3 2 1 NOTHING IN COMMON

Hanks versus Hanks. It had a familiar ring.

'You swear you won't make the same mistakes as your parents,' says Tom, 'but then you do.

'Samantha and I had so little common ground, it was just never meant to be. But at the time of my divorce I thought that all the bad things in my life were finally coming home to roost. I felt guilty that I was sentencing my own kids to the same sort of things I'd gone through at the same age.'

The divorce action was messy. Things had come to such a sorry state between the couple that a separate order was made by the divorce court to prevent either of them 'molesting, attacking, striking, threatening or otherwise disturbing the peace of the other'.

Hanks and Bess Armstrong have
Nothing in Common

The upshot of the bitter court battle that followed was that Tom was ordered to pay his wife around 20,000 dollars a month, plus about 1000 dollars for each of the children. Joint legal custody was agreed, although the court decreed that the children should stay with their mother.

Tom would be allowed to see Colin and Elizabeth on alternate weekends, but Samantha was given the exclusive rights to live in the Addison Street house. Tom had already moved out.

"Every day you wake up and ask yourself what is going on? What have I lost here? Why me?"

Later he said: 'You suddenly find yourself living in some jive hotel room for some three or four months, thinking that it is all totally bogus. Every day, you wake up and ask yourself: "What is going on? What have I lost here? Why me?"'

Tagging himself an emotional mess, Tom spent the one and only period of his life consulting a psychiatrist. 'I spent six months talking to him and, much to my amazement, felt a hell of a lot better at the end of it.'

In time, Samantha moved away to Sacramento with the children, while Tom returned to the North Hollywood home they had shared. In the meantime, the irony of his new film's title was doubtless not lost on him.

Called *Nothing in Common*, it paired him with TV comedy legend Jackie Gleason. Tom admits to being awed in the presence of the great man to begin with.

'But on the first day on set, Jackie came over to me and said: "How ya doin' kid? Let's make history." We threw our arms around each other and it was easy from then on.'

Unfortunately, the film itself made little history and was to be Gleason's last. He had cancer of the liver and died from it the following year.

Tom plays a high-flying girl chaser whose lack of communication with his parents (Gleason, Eva Marie Saint) forms the core of the movie. Tom confessed that he found 'rather too much of myself in the role. Some characters have nothing to do with you as a person. But just occasionally you find yourself drawing on your own experiences.'

Although the film lost less of its outlay than most of Hanks' vehicles of the mid Sixties, he clearly thought it time for a career reappraisal, instructing his agent not to offer him any more 'girl-chasing guys going nowhere.'

In reality, Tom was getting somewhere with a girl. Her name was Rita Wilson and she was soon to become his constant companion.

BOSOM BUDDIES

10 9 8 7 **6** 5 4 3 2 1

Tom and Rita had first met as co-stars of the 1985 flop *Volunteers*. Tom was attracted by her warm, stable personality, her sense of fun and her background, which was 100 times more well rooted than his own.

'Rita glowed with niceness,' says one of the film's co-stars, Xander Berkeley. 'You could tell they were fond of each other.'

'As soon as I met her,' remembers Tom, 'I knew I was in trouble. 'The attraction was there, but it made working more difficult. I believe that love at first sight does exist – but I now know you have to work at maintaining it. That's something you find out the hard way.'

Although Rita was engaged to someone else and Tom was immersed in endless divorce proceedings, they kept in touch. After her engagement was broken off, friendship turned to steady dating.

Right: A curious moment from **Dragnet**

On the set of **Nothing in Common**

With Dan Aykroyd in **Dragnet**

And there was another film in the offing. Taking second billing – a real rarity throughout his film career – Tom jumped at the chance of working with Dan Aykroyd in the pastiche of the old television series *Dragnet*. 'Dan and I met each other,' he says, 'and instantly knew we were going to have a blast making this movie. I never watched the show religiously as a kid, but I probably knew the theme tune before I could talk.

'And it's just a buddy buddy film. I don't have to jump in bed with a girl. That's sheer bliss!'

Tom plays Pep, the wild, off-the-wall partner of Aykroyd's staid sergeant Joe Friday. 'Between talking with Dan and making up a bunch of stuff myself, we managed to put this guy together,' he says.

Even if its satire gives way all too soon to comic-strip farce, the film was popular enough with the public and turned a handy profit. Hanks's personal notices were good and he was now on the verge of becoming a name the public would pay to see.

The relationship with Rita blossomed rapidly and they were married in 1988. A son, Chester (Chet) followed soon afterwards.

'I was really very immature and not very wise before I met Rita,' he says. 'I'm sure I was a difficult person to be in a relationship with. Thank God I had the good sense to woo her and wed her.

> ## "I was really very immature and not very wise before I met Rita."

'We had a lot of fights early on, but they were great, fabulous fights that we loved, fights that worked things out. She taught me an awful lot about being a better man, a better father and even a better actor. You know what? She taught me how to fight too!' Things were looking more settled all round on the Hanks marital front. Both Tom's parents were on their final marriages – Amos' third and Janet's fourth. And the children's income, Tom's especially, ensured that the continuing dialysis treatment needed for Amos's kidney problems could be comfortably covered.

Tom didn't know it, but his fee for making a film would soon triple. Coming his way was a project that had already been turned down by Harrison Ford, Jeff Bridges and Robert De Niro. None of them wanted to play a 12-year-old boy in a 35-year-old man's body.

Director Penny Marshall, who had worked with Tom on TV, knew he was perfect for the role. He was a lot cheaper than the other guys too. And he wanted the part. The studio bosses eventually agreed: Hollywood, and the world, was about to take Tom Hanks to its heart.

10 9 8 **7** 6 5 4 3 2 1

BIG TIME

There were several age-reversal comedies in the late eighties - *Vice-Versa, 18 Again!* and *Like Father, Like Son* are other examples. But *Big*, buoyed by Tom's infectious enjoyment of his role, was by far and away the most popular.

Fed up with being refused a ride on a fairground attraction because of his size, 12-year-old Josh Baskin goes to a weird 'make-a-wish' machine and tells it he wants to be big.

In the morning, he finds he has his wish, even if his pyjamas no longer fit. Driven from the house by his mother, who thinks he is his own kidnapper, Josh takes off after the travelling carnival and a speedy wish reversal.

Big. You know he's only twelve — see the angle of that right foot!

Previous page:
With Sally Field in **Punchline**

While he's searching, he lands a job with a toy company, where his childlike delight in his surroundings captivates the company boss (Robert Loggia) and earns him rapid promotion.

There's also a girl (Elizabeth Perkins), but when Josh takes her home, she's treated not to the night of passion she's expecting, but fun and games on a trampoline.

Despite falling in love with the girl, Josh, with the help of his friend Billy, eventually finds the wishing machine again and decides to go back to being a 12-year-old.

The childlike wonder Tom displays at his new life was skilfully done and extremely winning. The world's public responded with their feet and went to see the film in huge numbers.

'What I liked about *Big*,' said Tom, 'was that here was a film in which there were no car chases, no bad guys, no guns. We tried to make the whole thing very innocent.

'We didn't make Josh talk much. There's a lot of nodding and shrugging of shoulders in order for him to communicate. But that's how a kid of 12 going on 13 is going to behave.'

Although a sequence where Tom and Robert Loggia dance on giant toy piano keys is the one which sticks in most people's minds, another piece of comic 'business' sprang from the mind of Tom himself. Attending a party in a dinner suit more appropriate for a pantomime, Josh picks up a miniature sweet corn. Momentarily baffled by its size, he takes its measure for a moment before turning it sidewise and nibbling it delicately from end to end.

Although Tom had always enthused about working with actors such as Dan Aykroyd, John Candy and Jim Belushi, who had all come up from the late-night TV comedy route, they had all done one thing he had never tried – stand-up comedy. For his next movie, *Punchline*, Tom put that right.

He and Sally Field play aspiring club comedians who

become involved in a competition at a live TV audition, the winner to be given a featured spot on a prime-time show. Both stars spent three months to look like confident performers who could make audiences laugh. Tom worked the comedy clubs of Los Angeles and New York.

'When I first got up to do it,' he recalls, 'I knew I was going to be terrible – and I was. I was really bad. You're introduced as 'that funny guy from all those funny movies'. If you're not actually funny, it can get embarrassing very quickly.

'The first few times, I couldn't wait to get off the stage. I'd listen to tapes. I'd rewrite material. After about the ninth time, you feel slightly more comfortable. The three hardest jobs in America are coal mining, police work and stand-up comedy. I don't think I could make a living doing it.'

"Here was a film in which there were no car chases, no bad guys, no guns."

British critic Anne Billson was suffiently impressed to call Tom's performance 'extraordinary. Tom Hanks,' she wrote, 'is so manifestly superior to the rest of the comedians on display that it seems incredible that he hasn't already been snapped up for his own prime-time TV show.'

Although Tom's character is funny on stage, he's also cruel and self-centred. It was the first time he'd played such an unsympathetic character – yet in a way, life had prepared him for it. Says Sally Field, who would star with him again in *Forrest Gump*: 'he's very entertaining and amusing and easy to be around. But you know there's somebody else underneath, somebody dark. There's a sad side too. And that's what makes him so compelling on the screen.'

If Tom's work in *Punchline* probably cuts deeper than his child-adult in *Big*, it was for the latter film that he received his first Oscar nomination. Although it was no surprise when

Not the Oscar Acceptance Speech –yet!
A stand-up comedy scene from **Punchline**

Dustin Hoffman won the Academy Award best actor race that year for *Rain Man*, it was Tom who was voted best actor by the Los Angeles Film Critics for his combined work in *Big* and *Punchline*.

He himself described *Punchline* as a story about 'a very good stand-up comedian who is a horrible human being, and a wonderful human being who is a horrible stand-up comedian,' a simplification, perhaps, of two very complex characters.

Such versatility raised Tom's asking price per film from the $1 million of *Big* to more than three million. But it would be some time before his good judgment asserted itself again in terms of box-office success.

10 9 **8** 7 6 5 4 3 2 1

MAZES AND MONSTERS

Now that Tom was reading several scripts each month, it became increasingly difficult to make the right choice. Two he missed out on after the breakthrough of *Big* and *Punchline* were *Dead Poets Society* and *Field of Dreams*.

Tom, as ever, remained philosophical about turning down such massive hits. No one could have been better than Robin Williams, who eventually landed the lead in *Dead Poets Society*. But Tom would have been equally well suited to the Kevin Costner role in *Field of Dreams*. Tom, though, was to have the last laugh on Costner a few years later.

In the meantime, one he did accept, for a fee of $3,500,000, was *The 'Burbs*, a nightmare comedy about a group of home-obsessed suburbanites in a tight-knit neighbourhood who become consumed with curiosity about their oddball new neighbours.

With Carrie Fisher, deep in **The 'Burbs**

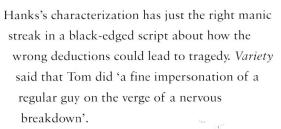

Hanks's characterization has just the right manic streak in a black-edged script about how the wrong deductions could lead to tragedy. *Variety* said that Tom did 'a fine impersonation of a regular guy on the verge of a nervous breakdown'.

'When you look at director Joe Dante's other films,' says Tom, 'you see this world which is completely pleasing on the surface. Yet deep down inside something horrible is going on. 'What made this black psycho-comedy so bizarrely interesting is that the stuff that goes on in real life in a regular neighbourhood will make your hair stand up on the back of your neck.'

Turner & Hooch was less interesting as a film, yet it made a bigger profit, largely on the appeal of the combination of Tom, as a fastidious cop, and the huge slobbery dog he is forced to take as a partner in a murder investigation. Tom is just beautiful as the house-proud sleuth who hoovers his partner's shirt-front in the car as the dog is messily eating a muffin.

Said Tom: 'It's the story of a man's life being completely rendered asunder by this dog. In some ways, it's the common man in an uncommon circumstance.'

Like other directors, Roger Spottiswoode was impressed by Tom's total absorption with the project. 'I never worked with an actor who is as much a film-maker,' he said, 'and who takes a great deal of responsibility for the film without being an interferer.'

Tom's career seemed to be steering itself smoothly through the maze of possible pitfalls. But he turned up a blind alley with *Joe versus the Volcano*. This failed fantasy-comedy-adventure begins well with Tom as a *1984*-type work slave and hypochondriac bamboozled into thinking he's dying from a 'brain cloud' so as to enmesh him in a hare-brained scheme. This involves his sailing off to a remote South Sea island where he's scheduled to end it all by jumping into a volcano.

Director John Patrick Shanley's screenplay has surprisingly little to offer after this, alas, apart from one or two good visual gags and Meg Ryan in three (equally forgettable) roles. Tom's special talents are wasted.

Never mind, Tom was assured that his next film, *The Bonfire of the Vanities*, would be a monster. It was, but not quite of the kind Tom had anticipated.

William Hurt had originally been slated for the lead in the screen version of Tom Wolfe's best-selling novel, and he would have been far more suited to the role than Tom Hanks.

"The stuff that goes on in real life in a regular neighbourhood will make your hair stand up on the back of your neck."

'I was aware that not everyone thought I was right to play Sherman McCoy,' said Tom. 'But when I was told it was me they wanted, I pursued it like I would any other job – losing just as much sleep and peeling my palms down to the bone about it.

'This is the story of a very shallow guy who attaches importance to things that just aren't important – a guy who has the world by the tail and thinks he can get away with having a mistress and even covering up a hit-and-run car accident. Sherman's not a nice man.'

It was clear that Tom could not really understand the public's reluctance to accept him in such a role, in the same way that, 40 years earlier, they would not have accepted James

With Rick Ducommun and Corey Feldman in **The 'Burbs**

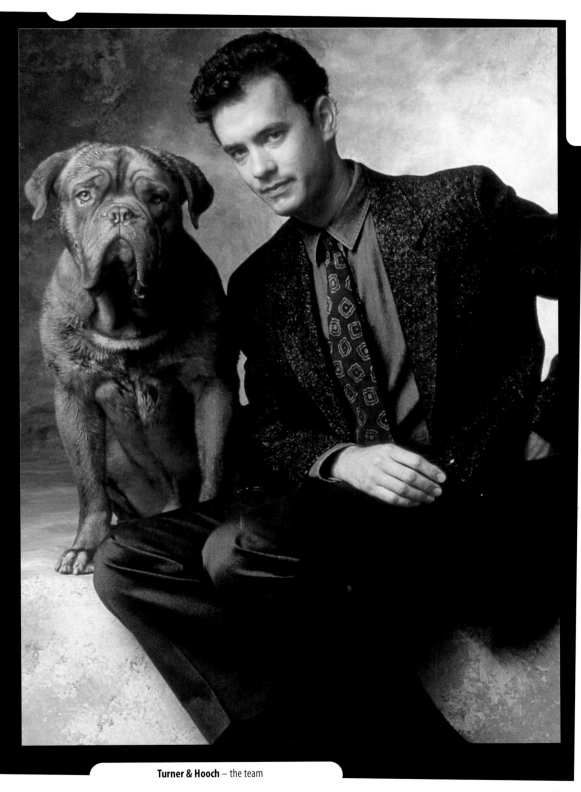

Turner & Hooch – the team

An alarming moment from **Splash**

Stewart as anything other than an upright guy. In a way, it was a compliment; but Tom was disappointed.

'The most amazing thing to me,' he said 'is the number of people who say that, because it's me playing him, he comes across as more sympathetic. Yet here's a guy who cheats on his wife, has a hideous job, has no relationship with his daughter whatsoever and lies to everyone he meets. How can he be sympathetic?'

"The most amazing thing to me is the number of people who say that, because it's me playing him, he comes across as more sympathetic."

In any case, the film was a turkey of Thanksgiving proportions. Not even having the courage to be faithful to its source material, the film was savaged by the critics and ignored by the public. Tom's notices were the worst of his career. It was undoubtedly the lowest ebb of his star days and he stayed away from the movies for 18 months.

'If you fail, as we did with *Bonfire*,' he says, 'it's very disappointing, but you can't run away. You have to stand up and say' "Yes, I made that movie, and it wasn't good".'

Honesty wasn't enough, though, to stop the good offers drying up like a plant that doesn't get watered.

'I learnt a bitter lesson from that experience,' Tom told an interviewer in 1992, as he hit the comeback trail. 'If you're going to make a film of a book that has entered a nation's consciousness, then do the book and don't change it.'

After he dabbled in direction, with an episode from the TV-film compilation of *Tales from the Crypt*, Tom received a further blow with the death of his father, Amos Hanks succumbing at last to the kidney problems that had plagued him for more than half his life.

Midway through 1992, though, Tom was offered a chance to revive his popularity by director Penny Marshall, who had made *Big*. It was a role originally suggested for Jim Belushi, and marked a complete departure from boyishness and charm for Tom – a bloated, bleary-eyed, has-been baseball coach in a film about wartime all-girl baseball teams called *A League of Their Own*.

'When Penny didn't want me to be romantic or attractive or cute,' says Tom, 'I was all for it. She wanted me to be as unattractive as possible. So she got me a bad haircut, and asked me to stop shaving and put on extra weight.

'I ate everything that was put in front of me and stacked on 25 pounds. I looked like a bull. I had rolls of fat on the back of my neck... I was really pleased! When we started shooting, I blew out my caps because of the character's constant tobacco spitting. I tell you, I sacrificed everything for the good of this movie.'

Of the director, he said: 'She knows how to get good stuff out of me. She wears me down, makes me mad and sometimes I want to slug her. But she's awfully good at what she does.'

A League of Their Own was a solid hit, and Tom was once again considered employable. The next film he chose was a simple romantic drama that reunited him with his *Joe versus the Volcano* co-star, Meg Ryan. No one expected too much from it. But it, and the films that followed, were to make Tom one of the most feted and powerful actors in the world.

Overleaf:
A League of Their Own:
Hanks co-stars with Madonna;
Rosie o'Donnell watches them clash

The Bonfire of the Vanities: Tom Hanks,
Melanie Griffith and Bruce Willis go up in smoke

A LEAGUE OF HIS OWN

10 9 8 7 6 5 4 3 2 1

A beguiling romance that pulls pretty well every emotional string, *Sleepless in Seattle* is a sweet and sometimes funny film about a young widower who pours his heart out to a radio agony aunt (at the instigation of his eight-year-old son), a plea that reaches the ears of the Ryan character, who's already engaged to someone else, and not destined to meet Tom until the last few seconds of the film.

'It's a simple movie,' says Tom, 'told within its confines and largely free of artifice. And I think audiences just responded to that. In order to enjoy most blockbuster hits these days, you've got to believe that dinosaurs can be genetically mutated, or that a guy in a bat-suit can drive through a city rounding up penguins.

Telephone talk in **Sleepless in Seattle**

Sleepless in Seattle – Hanks alone, but not for long

Big–making a mess

'Here, the only thing you have to believe is that two people can still fall in love. When you look at Hollywood movies these days, that's a fairly original concept. And the strength of the whole thing is that you have a sense of these two people together throughout the film. The fact that we don't really get together until the end – well, what better way to end the movie?'

Tom's wife Rita played a supporting role in the film. They were thinking of a second child now that they had settled into the Malibu Colony house they had bought from director John Frankenheimer in 1991, but it hadn't happened yet.

And the upswing in Tom's career was consuming ever larger chunks of his free time. Hardly had the dust settled on *Sleepless in Seattle*'s American take of $126 million than the film capital was abuzz with talk about Tom's controversial new role.

Sleepless in Seattle – the climax

A tender moment from **Philadelphia**

Sleepless in Seattle – Hanks and umbrella

In direct contrast to *A League of Their Own*, this time he had to shed more than two stone – to play a gay lawyer dying from AIDS.

Tom had first read the script for *Philadelphia* as far back as 1989, when it was still called *People Like Us*. 'I knew then,' he says, 'that I would give my right arm for the leading role. I'd almost always been Mr Nice Guy in the movies and that's precisely why I wanted to do it. I figured that if men and women liked me, they would still like me as a gay.

'So I read every book I could on AIDS. I talked to doctors, and people with AIDS.

'I went to see one man who was dying. We talked for hours, and he was giving me tips on how I would look, act and feel at various stages of the illness.

'He told me that when he was first diagnosed he went to the window and thought: "Clouds, this is the last time I'm going to see you". I thought about that when I did one scene in the film, and it brought tears to my eyes.

'When it was time to leave him, I gave him a hug. His body was like it was on fire: AIDS was eating him up. As I hugged him, I knew I had to make the film.'

Once again, though, the physical demands were frightening. 'I worked with a couple of sports doctors who usually beef actors up. I told them I wanted the exact opposite. They put me on a diet, with lunch that would fit in a teacup and the dinner on a saucer.

'I was impressed with his discipline,' says co-star Denzel Washington, who plays the lawyer who helps Tom pursue his claim for unfair dismissal against his law firm. 'The guy wasn't eating anything. He was just breathing air and taking

"I'd almost always been Mr Nice Guy in the movies and that's precisely why I wanted to do it."

Sleepless in Seattle, but communicating

Sacked from his job in **Philadelphia**

Tom with Robin Wright in **Forrest Gump**

in rice cakes. I think he was down to about 600 calories a day.

'I always had a pack of candy and stuff, and just put them in Tom's bag. He'd say: "Just let me smell the wrapper."'

Tom eventually shed around 30 pounds from his natural 170-pound frame. 'There was a particularly tough two-week period,' he recalls, 'when I was woozy from hunger. For a couple of days I couldn't stand up without grabbing a chair.'

He also had his hair progressively thinned as shooting went on. 'I wanted my hair to get gradually thinner and greyer, as it would. It helped my face look more drawn and angular as the story wore on. Towards the end of filming, though, I could hardly stand to look in the mirror because the face staring back at me was so depressing.'

Inevitably, the film itself courted controversy when it

opened to largely positive reviews. Although Tom had one headline-hitting clash with gay activists at the Berlin Film Festival, he said later that 'the gay community has reacted much in proportion to the rest of the audience. 'A third thinks we've done a truly wonderful thing. Another third thinks we've done a pretty good job, but that we weren't radical enough. And a third has loathed the film because it hasn't taken the stand it wanted.'

British critic Peter Cox described Tom's performance as 'quite brilliant'. Most American writers were equally impressed and an Oscar nomination was inevitable. This time Tom was a strong favourite to win.

One writer asked him what he'd say if he won the award. Tom replied that 'the important thing is to get on and get off without saying something that will embarrass you for the rest of your life.' He didn't make it. Tom won the award all right, but his speech of acceptance must go down as one of the two or three most cringe-making in history.

Clutching the Oscar, Tom rambled on for what seemed like ages, telling his global audience that 'I know my work in this case is magnified by the fact that the streets of Heaven are too crowded with angels.

'We know their names, they number a thousand for each one of the red ribbons that we wear here tonight. They finally rest in the warm embrace of the gracious Creator of us all, a healing embrace that cools their fever, that clears their skin and allows their eyes to see the

"The important thing is to get on and get off without saying something that will embarrass you for the rest of your life."

simple, self-evident common sense truth that is made manifest by the benevolent Creator of us all.

'It was written down on paper by wise men, tolerant men, in the city of Philadelphia 200 years ago. God bless you all. God have mercy on us all. God bless America.'

Well, it was different. Although one writer's contention that the Oscar-winner had 'blubbered wildly' was something of an exaggeration, Tom did admit that 'what happens is you get swept away with the emotion of the event. It's easy to forget exactly what you wanted to say under the circumstances.'

Never mind, one person who *was* cheering was his mother Janet. She had been flown in from her Red Bluff home by Tom for the ceremony. 'All the family,' she said, 'all the kids, everyone, gathered at Tom's house before the night of the awards, and we all took pictures.

'When he won the Oscar, I cried. It was like, despite everything, we were a family again, all of us. It was one of the happiest moments of my life.' One or two of the gay 'mentors' mentioned in Tom's speech were, however, it was reported, less than happy at being 'outed' by the star.

All of this, though, was to be overshadowed by Tom's next film, which would take more, much more, at the box-office than *Sleepless in Seattle* and *Philadelphia* put together. As Tom was also in for a percentage of the profits rather than a straight salary, *Forrest Gump* would also make him one of Hollywood's richest actors.

It was, on the surface, a simple story about a simple man, but its advanced special effects and the persuasiveness of a leading performance that gets under your skin triggered it into a blockbuster of amazing proportions. It also gave the world a new catchphrase: 'Life is like a box of chocolates. You never know what you're gonna get.'

Unquenchably cheerful, Forrest Gump is a backward boy from Alabama with an IQ of no more than 75. 'The script doesn't slap a label like disabled on him,' said Tom. 'He's just slow. He only has his common sense.'

This is enough, though, to see him through the Vietnam War, teach Elvis to swivel his pelvis, beat the Chinese with his table-tennis skills, accidentally alert the security forces to Watergate, join a TV chat show with John Lennon – and become a millionaire in the shrimp and computer industries.

Courtesy of movie trickery, he also meets three American presidents. 'For the table tennis scenes,' remembers Tom, 'all I did was stand there prancing around, waving two ping pong bats. Then they used video graphics to make the balls hit my bats. That was all so ridiculous it became great fun.

'I went from being a film craftsman on the one hand to, essentially, a trained chimpanzee on the other – just standing there, doing what I was told over and over again, and being rewarded by being allowed to go home.'

There was work for Hanks's younger brother Jim, with whom he had formed a much closer relationship than before – as his stand-in. Recalls Jim: 'I doubled for Tom in all the long-distance running shots of Forrest. I ran my butt off. But Tom knew no one could get the gangly Hanks run like I could.'

Forrest Gump took a cool $275 million at American cinemas, and much more around the world. It duly took the Academy Award as best film, while, as best actor, Tom claimed his second best actor Oscar in a row, a feat equalled only by Spencer Tracy more than 50 years earlier.

Forrest Gump in person

Unfortunately, Tom showed he had learned little from the acceptance speech disaster of the previous year. Once again overcome by the occasion, he began by thanking his wife Rita and people connected to the film, but then drifted off into a baffling babble in which he told those present that 'I feel as though I am standing on magic legs, in a special effects process shot that's too unbelievable to imagine and far too costly to make a reality.

'But here is my mark and there is where I am supposed to

look. And, believe me, the power and the pleasure and the emotion of this moment is a constant, the speed of light. It will never be diminished, nor will my appreciation and the meaning between two simple words that I can only offer you here. Thank you. God bless you in this room and God bless you all around the world.' Forrest Gump, for sure, would have kept it simpler.

Before moving on to the space-age drama of *Apollo 13*, Tom voiced the leading character – a toy cowboy called Woody – in the first completely computer-animated feature cartoon, Disney's *Toy Story*.

'Doing the voice of Woody was much harder than I ever anticipated it would be,' says Tom. 'For one thing, the pace is much faster than working on a regular film. There, you do a scene, then hang around for hours while they get ready to do the next. On this film, there were no stand-ins. You have to essentially act full-bore 100 per cent, standing there with your headphones on for three or four hours at a time.'

Although voice stars don't usually sell animated features, Tom's efforts can't have done the film any harm. It's made nearly $200 million to date in America alone. Strangely, Woody's nemesis in the film is a toy astronaut named Buzz Lightyear, voiced by Tim Allen, and much like the Major Matt Mason with whom Tom had played as a kid. A third astronaut was about to dominate his life for the next few months – but he was the real thing.

Hanks in pensive mood

10 987654321
A CAREER IN ORBIT

Hanks as Jim Lovell, Captain of the ill-fated **Apollo 13**

The role of Jim Lovell in the story of the ill-fated space mission of 1970 had, it had been said, long been coveted by Kevin Costner. Costner actually looked quite like Lovell. Lovell was said to be keen on the idea, too.

When the film came before the cameras in 1995, however, it was astro-nut, lifelong *Star Trek* fan and amateur astronomer Tom Hanks who had been picked to play the role.

The same Tom Hanks who had turned a film called *Field of Dreams* over to Costner six years earlier and let what might have been one of his biggest hits slip through his fingers.

'Jim Lovell was very good,' says Tom. He never mentioned Kevin Costner. In fact, he was probably a bit too good to me. He wanted to show me a bit of what being an astronaut and flyer was really like, so he took me up in his own plane.

I didn't expect to have to pilot the thing, but when we got up to 16,000 feet he asked me to take the controls. I was told to find two stars, Antares and Nunki, which some fighter pilots use to help their computer navigational systems. That was a disaster for a start.

'Then he pitched the plane over, causing my arms to float upwards. My stomach wasn't far behind. My mouth started watering and I was immediately bathed in sweat.

How could I tell my childhood hero that I felt sick? Thank God, somehow I got back to the ground without actually throwing up.'

Training at the NASA Space Center in Houston, Texas, was hardly more palatable for Tom and fellow 'astronauts' Kevin Bacon, Bill Paxton and Gary Sinise.

After 10 days inside a KC-135 jet, simulating weightlessness, the actors

'My mouth started watering and I was immediately bathed in sweat'.

nicknamed the plane *The Vomit Comet*. 'Being weightless,' said Tom, 'has a tendency to send everything in your stomach careering outwards.

'You're literally flying around, bouncing off walls and floating upside down. It gets so you feel very, very ill and hardly know where you are. I didn't actually throw up at all, but I felt so sick one day I could have sworn I was having a baby at 35,000 feet!'

None of this, of course, showed on screen. The actors' conviction as astronauts and director Ron Howard's skilful maintenance of suspense kept the film's tension on a high throughout, even though many of its older viewers, at least, must have known the outcome. After a crisis in outer space, the Moon mission is abandoned and the crew manages to make it back to earth. The film was quickly a number one box-office hit, running up total US takings of $172 million.

There was to be no Oscar for Tom this time, but he did have cause for celebration with the birth of his and Rita's second son, patriotically named Truman Theodore after two past presidents. And, after being 'in far too many religions', he and Rita became members of the Greek Orthodox Church.

Encouraged by the reviews for his work behind the cameras on the 1992 TV anthology *Tales from the Crypt* – *Variety* had said: 'Tom Hanks' directorial debut... clever and traditional... is a nifty piece of work' – Tom had for some time been working on a small-scale project he wanted to direct himself.

Finance was no problem for the world's most popular actor, and so *That Thing You Do!* went before the cameras early in 1996.

As well as writing and directing, Tom also played a featured role, in a story that reflected his own love of the Beatles and their era. It's about the members of a fictional rock group called The Wonders, who have the greatest summer of their lives in 1964 when one of their songs rockets to the top of the charts.

After that, there was the little matter of celebrating his 40th birthday.

Two months later, *That Thing You Do!* made its bow in American cinemas. Said *Variety*: 'The best thing to be said about Hanks' feature debut (as director) is that it bears all the elements that have made him a movie star: boyish charm, natural ease, comic precision and, above all, generosity of spirit.'

There was a cameo role in the film for Rita Wilson, and she almost stole the show with a warm and attractive performance as a sultry hostess in a bar.

Tom worked tirelessly on the film's behalf, travelling around America and Europe and appearing on endlesss TV talk shows. Critical reception was mixed but on the whole

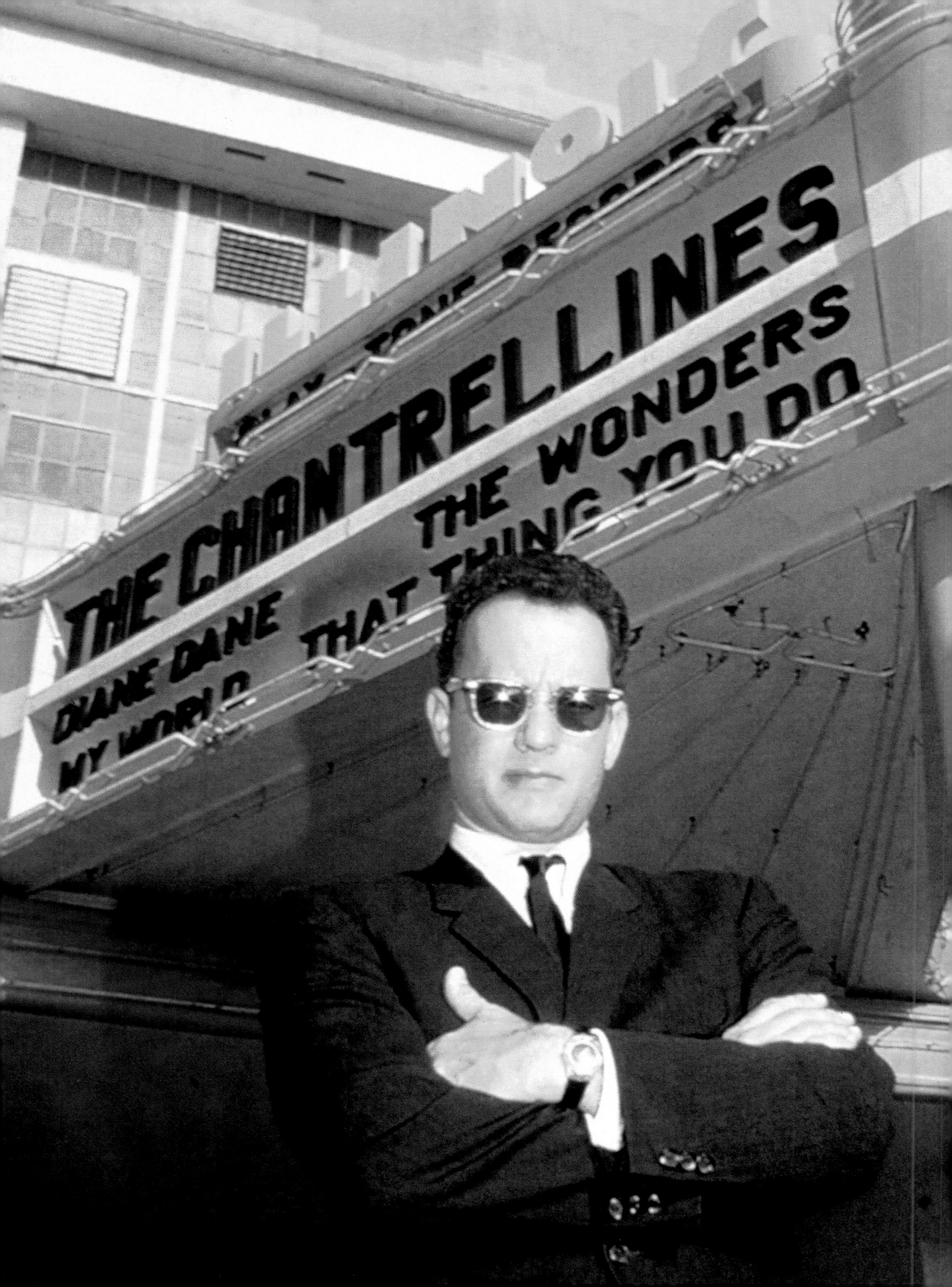
THE CHANTRELLINES
DIANE DANE
THE WONDERS

That Thing You Do: Hanks (left) and (above) with the fictitious Wonders

favourable. Tom's name in a supporting role undoubtedly added marque value, even if the role of the group's sharkishly smiling manager would probably have been better played by an actor like James Woods.

Ever the perfectionist, Tom was less than satisfied with the final results. 'There are so many things wrong with the film that I'd like to go back and do again. But it was a brutal, completely exhausting experience. I was in crisis 18 hours a day over the two months I was shooting and editing the movie. I now know I tried to do too much.'

Meanwhile, the world whetted its lips at the news that Tom and Steven Spielberg were in talks to film a screenplay called *Saving Private Ryan*. With the biggest-earning star and director teaming up, cinema managers could hear their tills ticking over already.

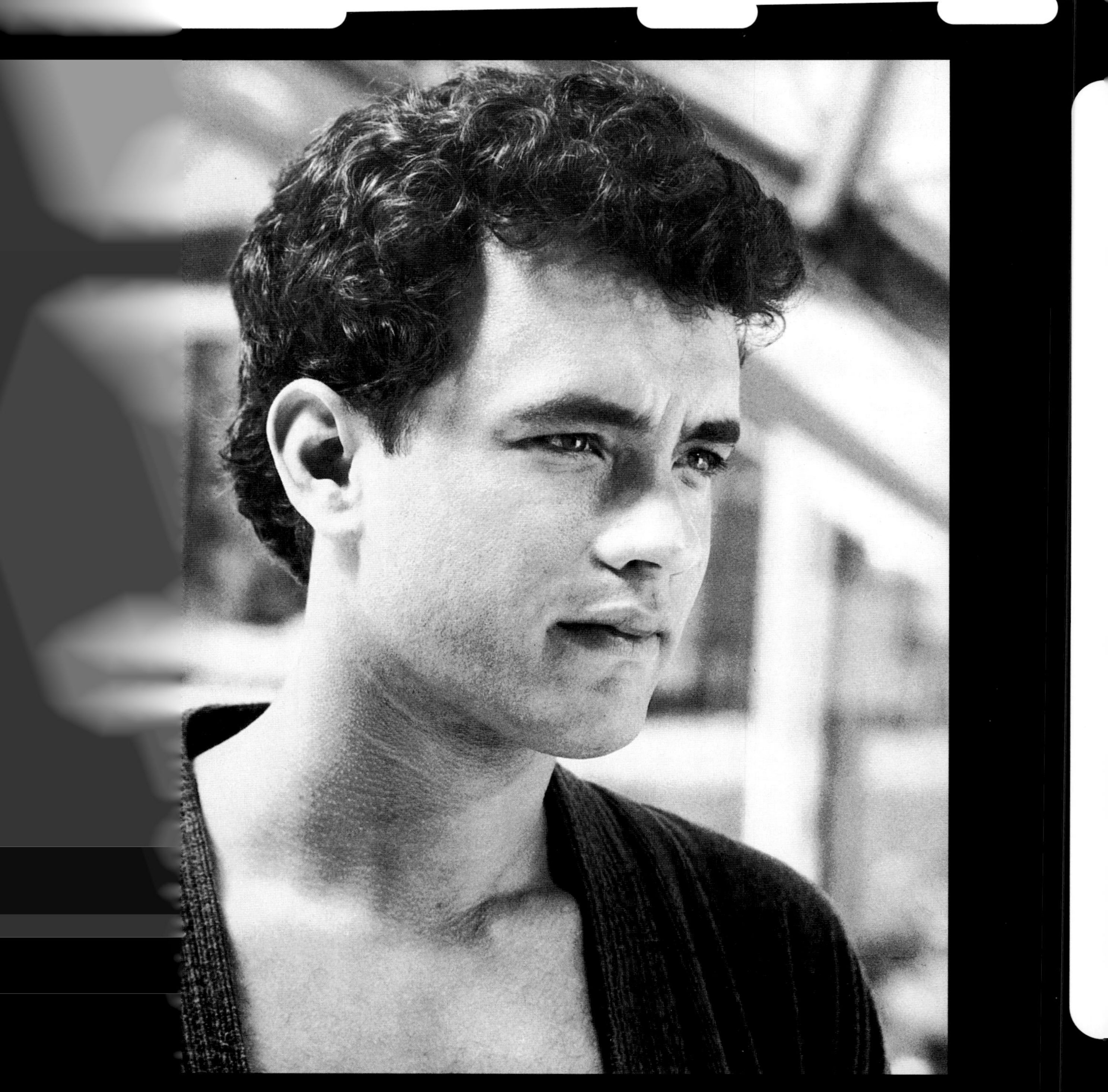

The big budget movie, about the efforts to rescue a hero soldier during World War Two, took Tom to locations in England and Ireland during the summer and autumn of 1997.

Little of this excitement seems to touch Tom's own lifestyle, very quiet by Hollywood standards. Says sister Sandra, now married to a Seychelles-born policeman and living in England: 'His idea of a big day out is a double-header at the Dodgers' baseball stadium, a diet coke and a hot dog. I mean, that's Tom.'

Hanks has a quiet lifestyle by Hollywood standards

Ever the sports fan, Tom has added surfing and basketball to his other passions. Says brother Jim: 'It's very hard to know what to buy Tom Hanks for his birthday, so I bought him a basketball. He'd got a new basketball hoop at home and I knew it was what he wanted. He kept saying: "Man, this is great".'

And Tom is well aware that his 'ordinary Joe' qualities have made his fortune. 'What you see is what you get,' he has said. 'I'm not threatening. I'm not a wife-stealer. Not much gets on my nerves, and I've only had my Tarot cards read once. That makes me a bit of an oddball in this town.

'I guess the movies I do show that it's possible to be ordinary and still do extraordinary things.' It's a motto that might apply to his own life.

'I had a cab driver a long time ago,' Tom reflects, 'an older black man. He just seemed to be one of the most contented, decent people I'd ever had the chance to chat with. He also looked incredibly young.

'He told me he had grandchildren, so I asked him how he stayed so young. He replied: "Well, I tell you, I tries to entertain no worries". It occurred to me that that was the secret of living, right there. I probably have most of the worries everyone else does, but I just try not to worry too much. It's a good lesson.'

FILMOGRAPHY

HE KNOWS YOU'RE ALONE (1980)

Director: Armand Mastroianni 92 mins

Don Scardino (Marvin), Caitlin O'Heaney (Amy), Elizabeth Kemp (Nancy), Tom Rolfing (Killer), Lewis Arlt (Len), Patsy Pease (Joyce), James Rebhorn (Prof. Carl), Tom Hanks (Elliot)

Issued on MGM/UA Video

MAZES AND MONSTERS / RONA JAFFE'S MAZES AND MONSTERS (1982)

Director: Steven H Stern 93 mins

Tom Hanks (Robbie), Wendy Crewson (Kate), David Wallace (Daniel), Chris Makepeace (Jay Jay), Lloyd Bochner (Hall), Vera Miles (Cat), Anne Francis (Ellie), Susan Strasberg (Meg)

Not issued on video

SPLASH (1984)

Director: Ron Howard 110 mins

Tom Hanks (Allen Bauer), Daryl Hannah (Madison), John Candy (Freddie Bauer), Eugene Levy (Dr Kornbluth), Dody Goodman (Mrs Stimler), Shecky Greene (Buyrite), Richard B Shull (Dr Ross), Bobby DiCicco (Jerry)

Issued on Walt Disney Home Video

BACHELOR PARTY (1984)

Director: Neal Israel 106 mins

Tom Hanks (Rick Gassko), Tawny Kitaen (Debbie), Adrian Zmed (Jay), George Grizzard (Thompson), Barbara Stuart (Mrs Thompson), Robert Prescott (Cole), Michael Dudikoff (Ryko), Wendie Jo Sperber (Tina)

Issued on CBS/Fox Video

VOLUNTEERS (1985)

Director: Nicholas Meyer 107 mins

Tom Hanks (Lawrence Bourne), John Candy (Tom Tuttle), Rita Wilson (Beth Wexler), Tim Thomerson (John Reynolds), Gedde Watanabe (At Toon), Xander Berkeley (Kent), Allan Arbus (Albert), Clyde Kusatsu (Souvanna)

Issued on Warner Home Video

THE MAN WITH ONE RED SHOE (MISCHIEF) (1985)

Director: Stan Dragoti 95 mins

Tom Hanks (Richard), Lori Singer (Maddy), Dabney Coleman (Cooper), Carrie Fisher (Paula), Jim Belushi (Morris), Charles Durning (Ross), Edward Herrmann (Brown), Tom Noonan (Reese)

Issued on CBS/Fox Video

THE MONEY PIT (1985)
Director: Richard Benjamin 91 mins

Tom Hanks (Walter Fielding), Shelley Long (Anna), Maureen Stapleton (Estelle), Alexander Godunov (Max), Joe Mantegna (Art), Philip Bosco (Curly) Josh Mostel (Jack), Carmine Caridi (Brad Shirk)

Issued on CIC Video3

EVERY TIME WE SAY GOODBYE (1986)
Director: Moshe Mizrahi (98 mins)

Tom Hanks (David), Cristina Marsillach (Sarah), Benedict Taylor (Peter), Anat Atzmon (Victoria), Gila Almagor (Lea), Monny Moshaniv (Nessim), Caroline Goodall (Sally), Esther Parnass (Rosa)

Issued on Vestron Video

NOTHING IN COMMON (1986)
Director: Garry Marshall 119 mins

Tom Hanks (David Basner), Jackie Gleason (Max Basner), Eva Marie Saint (Lorraine Basner), Hector Elizondo (Charlie), Barry Corbin (Andrew), Bess Armstrong (Donna), Sela Ward (Cheryl Ann), John Kapelos (Roger)

Issued on RCA/Columbia Pictures Video

DRAGNET (1987)
Director: Tom Mankiewicz 106 mins

Dan Aykroyd (Joe Friday), Tom Hanks (Pep Streebek), Christopher Plummer (Rev Jonathan Whirley), Alexandra Paul (Connie Swail), Harry Morgan (Cannon), Jack O'Halloran (Muzz), Elizabeth Ashley (Jane), Dabney Coleman (Caesar)

Issued on CIC Video

BIG (1988)
Director: Penny Marshall 102 mins

Tom Hanks (Josh Baskin), Elizabeth Perkins (Susan), Robert Loggia (Mac), John Heard (Paul Davenport), Jared Rushton (Billy), Jon Lovitz (Scotty), Mercedes Ruehl (Mrs Baskin), David Moscow (Young Josh)

Issued on CBS/Fox Video

PUNCHLINE (1988)
Director: David Seltzer 128 mins

Sally Field (Lilah Krytsick), Tom Hanks (Steven Gold), John Goodman (John Krytsick), Mark Rydell (Romeo), Kim Griest (Madeline Urie), Damon Wayans (Percy), Paul Mazursky (Arnold), Barry Neikrug (Krug)

Issued on RCA/Columbia Pictures Video

FILMOGRAPHY

THE 'BURBS (1989)

Director: Joe Dante 103 mins

Tom Hanks (Ray Peterson), Bruce Dern (Mark), Carrie Fisher (Carol), Rick Ducommun (Art), Corey Feldman (Ricky), Henry Gibson (Dr Klopek), Wendy Schaal (Bonnie), Courtney Gains (Hans Klopek)

Issued on CIC Video

TURNER & HOOCH (1989)

Director: Roger Spottiswoode 97 mins

Tom Hanks (Scott Turner), Mare Winningham (Emily Carson), Craig T Nelson (Hyde), Reginald VelJohnson (Sutton), Scott Paulin (Zack Gregory), JC Quinn (Boyett), John McIntire (Amos Reed), Beasley (Hooch)

Issued on Buena Vista Home Video

JOE VERSUS THE VOLCANO (1990)

Director: John Patrick Shanley 100 mins

Tom Hanks (Joe Banks), Meg Ryan (DeDee/Angelica/Patricia), Robert Stack (Dr Ellison), Lloyd Bridges (Graynamore), Dan Hedaya (Waturi), Ossie Davis (Marshall), Amanda Plummer (Dagmar, Carol Kane (Hairdresser)

Issued on Warner Home Video

THE BONFIRE OF THE VANITIES (1990)

Director: Brian De Palma 125 mins

Tom Hanks (Sherman McCoy), Bruce Willis (Fallow), Melanie Griffith (Maria), Kim Cattrall (Judy), Saul Rubinek (Jed Kramer), Morgan Freeman (Judge White), F Murray Abraham (Abe Weiss), Rita Wilson (PR woman)

Issued on Warner Home Video

RADIO FLYER (1992)
Director: Richard Donner 113 mins

Elijah Wood (Mike), Lorraine Bracco (Mary), Joseph Mazzello (Bobby), Adam Baldwin (Stepfather), John Heard, Ben Johnson, Tom Hanks (Older Mike/Narrator)

Issued on Columbia/Tri-Star Home Video

TALES FROM THE CRYPT (1992)
Directors: Tom Hanks, Robert Longo, William Friedkin 75 mins

Cast for TH's episode, 'None But the Lonely Heart': Treat Williams, Frances Sternhagen, Henry Gibson, Sugar Ray Leonard, Tom Hanks, Clive Rosengren, Bibi Osterwald

Issued on Warner Home Video

A LEAGUE OF THEIR OWN (1992)
Director: Penny Marshall 128 mins

Tom Hanks (Jimmy Dugan), Geena Davis (Dottie Hinson), Lori Petty (Kit Keller), Madonna (Mae Mordabito), Bill Pullman (Bob Hinson), Rosie O'Donnell (Doris), Jon Lovitz (Cappy), David Strathairn (Ira)

Issued on Columbia/Tri-Star Home Video

FALLEN ANGELS (1993)
Directors: Phil Joanou, Tom Hanks, Steven Soderbergh 92 mins

Cast for TH's episode, 'I'll Be Waiting': Bruno Kirby, Marg Helgenberger, Dan Hedaya, Jon Polito, Peter Scolari, Tom Hanks, Dick Miller

Issued (separately) on Polygram Video. TH's episode: 30 mins

SLEEPLESS IN SEATTLE (1993)

Director Nora Ephron 105 mins

Tom Hanks (Sam Balwin), Meg Ryan (Annie Reed), Ross Malinger (Jonah), Bill Pullman (Walter), Victor Garber (Greg), Rosie O'Donnell (Becky), Rita Wilson (Suzy), Carey Lowell (Maggie)

Issued on Columbia/Tri-Star Home Video

PHILADELPHIA (1993)

Director: Jonathan Demme 122 mins

Tom Hanks (Andrew Beckett), Denzel Washington (Joe Miller), Jason Robards (Wheeler), Mary Steenburgen (Belinda Conine), Antonio Banderas (Miguel), Ron Vawter (Bob), Charles Napier (Judge), Joanne Woodward (Sarah)

Issued on Columbia/Tri-Star Home Video

FORREST GUMP (1994)

Director: Robert Zemeckis 142 mins

Tom Hanks (Forrest Gump), Robin Wright (Jenny), Gary Sinise (Dan), Sally Field (Mrs Gump), Mykelti Williamson (Bubba), Kirk Ward (Earl), Calvin Gadsden (Sgt Sims), Elizabeth Hanks (School bus girl)

Issued on CIC Video

TOY STORY (1995)

Director: John Lasseter 80 mins

Voices: Tom Hanks (Woody), Tim Allen (Buzz), Don Rickles (Potato Head), Jim Varney (Slinky Dog), Wallace Shawn (Rex), John Ratzenberger (Hamm), Annie Potts (Bo Peep), R Lee Ermey (Sergeant)

Issued on Buena Vista Home Video

APOLLO 13 (1995)
Director: Ron Howard 140 mins

Tom Hanks (Jim Lovell), Kevin Bacon (Swigert), Bill Paxton (Haise), Gary Sinise (Mattingly), Kathleen Quinlan (Marilyn Lovell), Ed Harris (Krantz), David Andrews (Conrad), Xander Berkeley (Hurt)

Issued on CIC Video

THAT THING YOU DO (1996)
Director: Tom Hanks 106 mins

Tom Everett Scott (Guy), Jonathon Schaech (Jimmy), Liv Tyler (Faye), Steve Zahn (Lenny), Ethan Embry (Bass player), Tom Hanks (Mr White), Charlize Theron (Tina), Alex Rocco (Sol Silver), Kevin Pollak (Vic Koss), Peter Scolari (Troy), Rita Wilson (Marguerite)

Issued on CBS/Fox Video

SAVING PRIVATE RYAN (1998)
Director: Steven Spielberg

Tom Hanks, Edward Burns, Adam Goldberg, Matt Damon, Jeremy Davies, Tom Sizemore, Van Diesel, Barry Pepper, Giovanni Ribisi

Distributed by UIP/Paramount

INDEX